MAPMAKERS VS OPAQUERS

Organisational digital technology projects need a clear map

Karl Jeffery
Dimitris Lyras

Software for Domain Experts Ltd

MAP MAKERS VS OPAQUERS - AND HOW TO MAKE DIGITAL PROJECTS WORK

CONTENTS

MAPS AND DIGITAL PROJECTS

Digital projects for organisations go well when there is a clear map of what the technology will do to support the organisation's goals and how it will get there.

Digital projects fail when they are opaque - people don't understand why the technology is there, what it is meant to do to help them, and how it will do that.

We need more map makers – and also we need map makers who understand the forces which make technology opaque, and be ready to take them on.

Map making should be great fun, if you like working with people to figure out how things work and how to make them better

DIGITAL PROJECTS WITH A CLEAR MAP ARE MORE LIKELY TO WORK

Digital projects for organisations can be more successful when they have clearer maps for what the technology does, and how it dovetails with what the organisation and its decision makers and experts do.

In this book. we suggest ways you can do it, and explain some of the obstacles which will come in your way as you try. How to identify them and, in some cases, fight them.

Many digital projects for organisations are not successful. The main reason for this may be that the people involved don't have a clear understanding, or map, of what the technology is supposed to do, and how it is supposed to achieve that.

Typically, companies buy technologies as a number of different 'products' which they expect to work together to give them what they need, rather than implement technologies according to an integrated plan.

We could use an analogy of someone who builds their home by putting together a number of different 'products'. They might start with something small and cheap, like a caravan, and then gradually build on it – a garden, a driveway, an extra building or two from concrete blocks, water and electricity supply, an out-side toilet. If they find they have money to spare, they may buy something fancy like a jacuzzi.

There are people who seem to have built their homes in this way. But most of us live in homes planned in an integrated way, with all the components designed around a goal of giving us maximum comfort and convenience for the space and resources available, drawing on experience from houses which have been built before.

Similarly, the most effective organisational digital technology would be built according to an integrated plan to achieve the core goals and drawing on past experience.

This building analogy only goes so far for organisational digital projects, because organisations are rarely planning digital technology from a blank sheet of paper, as a building architect can. But map making is just as relevant when there is a lot of digital technology which already exists. You can make maps of how everything fits together, identify where it does and doesn't align with organisational goals, and where improvements can be made.

Map making can be about connecting together the maps which already exist, such as the maps held in the minds of the organisational leaders and its decision makers for achieving organisational goals, how the existing digital projects have been designed, and the maps which underly the development of commercial software products.

Map making is about communications, more than about finding paths. We all make maps in our minds about what we want to do, which we don't necessarily share with others. But for digital projects for organisations, we do need to share them.

Mapmaking is also about being aware of the opposing forces which bring opacity to organisational digital projects, preventing people from understanding what is going on. We can often see it as a battle between mapmakers and opacity-creators (who we call 'opaquers'). This book sets out how the map makers can win.

WHAT ORGANISATIONAL TECHNOLOGY IS FOR – WE SAY SITUATION AWARENESS

If we are going to make maps of how the goals of digital technology align with the goals of the organisation, we need to agree on what the goals of the digital technology are.

There are many possible goals of organisational digital technology. Some technologies are designed to automate work done by people, or reduce the amount of work which must be done in dangerous places. Some technologies are designed to support process optimisation, so everybody performs complex tasks in a structured, repeatable and optimised way. Some technologies share data in ways which were not available before. Some technologies support organisational management systems and drive new business models.

We propose a simple answer to this question, which incorporates nearly all of the above – to say,
the ultimate role of organisational digital technology is to support people's situation awareness and decision making.

Then, going through the examples above, you can see that technology can support situation awareness by automating easier aspects of a task so a person can focus more on oversight or complex aspects of the task (no automation system can automate an entire organisational process, there is always a person at the top).

It can support situation awareness by enabling someone to get the same level of awareness when they do a task remotely as they would when physically being there, as in flying an aircraft or operating an oil platform control system remotely.

It can support decision making by helping people understand what the company's procedures say should be done in this situation, in order to guide the person to do the task most effectively.

And it can support decision making by giving you the best available data, through better data communication and sharing.

All organisations, and most individuals working in them, have goals, such as more sales, less accidents, more production, less CO_2 emission, or doing what they have to do more efficiently or effectively.

These goals are set by the senior leaders, and rolled out to the experts who make decisions throughout the organisation. They use digital technology to get better situation awareness so they make better decisions.

To agree with this perspective, you would need to agree that the success of organisations comes down largely to the quality of decisions made by people within them. Not everybody agrees with this, some people believe that success of organisations comes down to their systems and business models. If you are one of these people, then you will not recognise the value of this book. You won't see the value of clear maps for technology.

WHAT OPACITY MEANS IN DIGITAL PROJECTS

When digital projects do not have clear maps, we can say they are opaque. People who work in the organisation don't understand how the technology can help them reach their goals, and how it can do what it promises to do.

This means that decision makers are less likely to support it, and it means that digital technology does far less than it could do, to support our organisations to do a good job.

The technology industry often uses phrases like "resistance to change" when people seem reluctant to take on new technology. Perhaps often, what this really means is, people don't see the point of it.

The domain experts are presented with technology "products" – packages of code, services, data storage, hardware – with big promises attached, such as that it is a maintenance or financial management system.

These products can rarely make a big contribution to an organisation by themselves, no matter how sophisticated they are, because they would need to be configured to give someone exactly what they need in order to do that, and every domain expert's role and needs are a little different.

Often we need an additional layer between technology products, which gather and manipulate data, and the digital services which give domain experts what they need to see, carefully mapped against their needs.

LAYERS OF MAP MAKING

The map of digital technology for organisations has multiple layers, giving different views to different people.

At the top we have the overall goals of the organisation and what it wants to achieve or improve, as set and reviewed by the senior leaders.

These goals are broken down to the goals of the individuals in the organisations who make decisions, who we call "domain experts".

Then we have the information and digital tools these domain experts need to better make decisions, understanding what is going on.

Then we have the digital technology which drives this. This can include various technology services and products which contribute to this situation awareness.

This is a very simplified picture, there are many other components, such as where one domain expert gets awareness of what someone else is doing in the company, and the willingness of investors and others to fund the development of technology products.

For digital technology to work for organisations, the map needs to be clear to everybody and aligned.

WE NEED MAP MAKERS

We need more people who can work out, and explain to others, how technology can best help an organisation, and its domain experts, to achieve its goals, and how it works to do that.

Technology map making is a difficult but learnable skill. It is similar to other organisational roles where someone figures out how to do something and explains it to others, such as a project manager does in any domain, or a building architect does.

The goal of this book is to give you some pointers for how to do it, how you can learn it, and how you can better spot the forces which oppose clear mapmaking.

If you are the kind of person who likes to understand how the working world works, enjoys doing things with technology (perhaps more than you enjoy technology itself), enjoys working with people, solving problems and connecting things together in new ways, map making can be great fun.

DOMAINS WHERE MAP MAKING WOULD BE MOST USEFUL

Digital mapmaking would be most useful in domains where there is complex decision making and judgement, with many different variables involved, and potential for digital systems to do more. Domains we have looked at include cybersecurity, all government services, decarbonisation, shipping company management, oil and gas production, financial services.

For example, organisational cybersecurity is becoming far more about map making than any individual "point" technology, because there are many different routes of attack which all need to be monitored with different technologies. Attackers look for a route where a company's defences are weakest, so companies need to monitor all the different attack routes. With an effective map, it would be possible to monitor the available data about all of the different attack routes, and see where attention should be focussed.

Decarbonisation efforts could benefit from map making, if we define the problem as working out how to do what we need to do in our businesses while minimising carbon impact, rather than seeking single 'point' solutions, such as hydrogen cars. As we make decisions in our business lives we can see what the carbon impacts of the various choices are, and we could monitor the carbon impact of these decisions on a daily basis.

Cancer treatment could benefit from better digital mapmaking, if the problem is defined as being able to better determine if someone has cancer, the sort of cancer it is, and how to treat it, drawing on the strengths of both human expertise and the vast databases of information about past cancers, bearing in mind every cancer has unique features about it.

Map making could help government organisations to function more effectively in general, achieving goals with less resources. This makes for a better society overall – whether the government organisation's role is to reduce crime, suppress viruses, or reach environmental targets.

Business agility in general would be improved from better map making, because it would support technologies which can give the different domain experts exactly what they need to understand how their domain is changing, and every domain is unique. Other general benefits include the creation of more interesting jobs, which support people's learning. It could help organisations feel less complex, both for their employees and their customers.

FORCES FOR OPACITY

Considering how confusing many people find organisational digital projects, we can say that the forces for opacity often come out on top.

One of the biggest forces for opacity is packaging of digital technology into 'products' or 'solutions'. This is done for commercial reasons, because vendors want to get the message across that a customer can solve a specific problem using this product. But it has the effect of shutting down a discussion about what this product actually is or does, which people need if they are going to understand how it can help them.

Talking about technology in terms of products has worked fine for many technology companies for years, so it is a method people want to stick with. But as digital technology gets more pervasive in our organisations, with decision makers expected to engage more deeply with it, the weakness of the product-centric approach gets more apparent.

A company may be sold a "customer relationship management" system. The biggest function it might achieve for the organisation, specifically, is manage contact details of customers, and enable customers to create tickets for support requests, which can be answered in a structured way.

This is a useful service from technology, but is perhaps not best understood by people if it is presented as a comprehensive system for managing customer relationships, which involve much more than contact details and support requests.

The company may be sold financial management software. This will do a good job of keeping track of transactions, customer and supply details, and funds in the bank account. But there are elements of financial management where it will do nothing to help, such as determining whether someone' s expenses submission is reasonable, or whether the company is receiving all the funds it agreed customers would transfer.

The company may be sold cybersecurity software. This may do a good job of scanning all the files to see if they contain known viruses before they can be opened on a company computer. It will not do anything to detect whether people using company computer networks are the individuals authorised to do the job they are undertaking, rather than just checking access rights.

Companies may have been persuaded to make a "data lake", putting all of their data in a large repository. There can be benefits expected from doing this from a digital systems development perspective, if it makes data easier for other systems to access. But this may not be a benefit which any domain expert, concerned with organisational goals rather than technological goals, will readily understand. It may actually make it harder for a domain expert to work with the data, if the process of moving data into a lake strips the data of its context.

These technology products may have been originally developed for a different company, with different goals. So they were designed around a map which is totally different to the technology map of the company the products are now being sold to.

If, as a digital map maker, you argue with the technologists that their map is not exactly what the organisation needs, they may use their advantage in technological competence to show organisation leaders that they are the people who should be listened to.

A TIMELESS DEBATE

These are modern challenges, but can be seen as a continuation of other debates, or battles, between clarity and opacity, which are a timeless theme of human existence.

For example, the UK's Economist magazine was set up in 1843 to "take part in a severe contest between intelligence, which presses forward, and an unworthy, timid ignorance obstructing our progress" – a purpose which is just as relevant in the 2020s.

Vaclav Havel, Czech president from 1989 to 2003 is attributed to the quote "Keep the company of those who seek the truth, and run away from those who have found it".

The words are different, but the theme is the same – life as an endless conflict between people who seek to continually develop and share more understanding about how the world works, and people whose intentions and actions obstruct this understanding, perhaps because their primary concern is protecting the existing state of affairs.

WHAT DIGITAL MAP MAKING MEANS

GOOD MAP MAKING EXAMPLES

In the world outside technology, there are examples everywhere of clear map making, and people with good map making skills.

Organisational leaders, and other communicators and educators such as teachers, journalists, and politicians, have learned to explain goals, what is necessary to reach the goals, and how what we are doing helps us to get there.

In these domains, there are established systems for judging how good individuals are at map making. While people who are not excellent map makers may stay in their jobs, because good mapmakers are very rare, the systems can ensure the strongest map makers are in the most important or prestigious roles, such as working as national leaders or journalists for the most important news outlets.

A good politician can explain what needs to be done and why it is important, in terms of the direct goals and priorities of individuals living in that country. This is an example of sharing a map.

A good lawyer can show why it is clear that a certain outcome needs to happen, in terms of the priorities of a good society, and why the evidence and other information supports this outcome being correct. In other words showing why the best map leads to the lawyer's desired outcome.

Building architects master the skill of mapping the best path through the various options available, trying to come up with a design their clients want for acceptable cost, considering the space and regulatory restrictions. Then they explain this map to others, with presentations, models, drawings and other methods.

In the digital world, examples of technology which has a clear map, mapped to what customers need, could include just about anything from Amazon and Apple – although bear in mind these are mainly products for individuals, not organisations. Microsoft has a leading role in organisational digital technology map making, but does not usually engage with domain experts on an individual level, leaving a large part of the map making to its partner companies.

THE ESSENCE OF THE MAP MAKING SKILL

The essence of the map maker's skill is this remarkable ability we have, as people, to figure out how complex things work and explain it to others.

This has been part of people's survival skillset since prehistoric times, when we needed the ability to understand the changing dynamics of our tribe, including who was on our side and who was working against us, even when motivations were hidden. Evolutionary scientists have suggested that the reason our brains became so large, compared to other animals, is because our social groups were much larger and more complex, so there was much more we needed to model and map.

Digital map makers need skills which prehistoric people did not require – an understanding and basic competence of digital technology.

As a map maker, you don't necessarily need to be highly technical – the skillset for programming and systems development is different, and that can be left to others. It is more important to be able to understand the organisation itself and its goals. For example if you are working with police technology, you will need to understand how a police department works,

It will help if you like people, enjoy working with people, and you enjoy learning about how people work, decide, plan, and use information. It will help if you are someone other people would welcome having a conversation with.

You need to be ready for the battle against the opaquers, helping maintain an organisational culture orientated towards map making.

MAP CONNECTING

Digital map making is not just about explaining technology, or figuring out how to implement it.

Some of the map making is actually map-connecting - connecting together the various separate maps held by budget holders, domain experts, technology companies and their investors about how organisation technology should work, commercially as well as technically.

Some of the map making is determining the maps which people already have in their minds of what they need (a process we might also call 'modelling'), such as the mental model a car driver has about what they need to know when driving. Digital technology needs to map against this.

Some of the map making is connecting different technology products, when we bring together the various information sources together, perhaps on a dashboard with an alerts system, so it can best help someone in a specific role to make better decisions.

Technology map making includes understanding technology products and software companies, including their map of motivations, what they are likely to do over time. How important certain customers are to a software vendor, and how much they would be willing to customise products to meet customer requests. The risks to the customer over time such as from being tied to a vendor, or having a vendor which refuses to integrate products with those of other software companies.

Digital map makers may need to work out how the maps of different software products can fit together to make the overall map. For example, making the right choice between large and small software companies. Small software companies may offer more flexibility, but working with them means challenges integrating products and services together, and more onus on the customer to vet products. A large software company will probably have already solved that, at least for their own products and services.

DIFFERENT LEVELS OF MAP MAKING

People in different roles of an organisation engage with the technology map in different ways.

You have budget holders and senior leaders in the organisation, who want to see specific goals achieved, such as improving performance and safety. They have a map of how they want to get there, and they want to ensure spending on digital technology, and anything else, helps achieve these goals.

You have the people who use the technology to make decisions, such as about purchasing, planning, risks and other operations, who we call the domain experts. They have maps for how they work which the software needs to align with.

You have people involved in the digital technology itself, in a variety of roles, including project managers, IT staff and software developers. They need to understand the map of how the technology is built, its goals, and how it aligns with everything else.

You have all the pre-existing, or 'legacy' digital technology in the organisation which people still need to work with. When we have to work with this, and integrate new systems with it, it helps a great deal if we understand why products were built the way they were, or the map behind them.

People working at a software company will have maps as part of their products - what they think organisations need, how their products serve that need, and how that product is built.

Software investors are also stakeholders. They have maps in their minds of which products organisations will want to buy. They will invest in software development which maps against this.

DIGITAL TECHNOLOGY ROLES AND MAPMAKING

People who work with digital technology are not necessarily good map makers.

People involved in programming, fixing technology problems and other deep dive roles are good at fine grained logic, and patient enough to get what is needed from a computer processor. But they do not necessarily have the abstraction and people skills for map making.

People in more senior CIO roles would not necessarily have had to get a detailed understanding of how the organisation, and technology, works to reach the level of map making we talk about here. Their competence may only extend as far as knowing how to implement specific products.

People with a background in user interface and user experience design will have done some work with process mapping, but this would probably not have included much requirement to understand how the organisation works, only how the user thinks through the interaction with the software.

If the user interface is for gathering information in an online form, for example, a user interface designer would consider how to make the form clear, but not consider what purpose the information in the form serves in the organisation. Why someone would be motivated to fill in the form, what happens if the form is not filled in, and the wider implications from the information in the form, such as a mortgage application used to determine whether a mortgage is agreed.

Software architecture is typically a highly technical role focussing on how software products and services integrate together – but does not usually require much understanding of the map of the organisation itself and its domain experts.

CONNECTING POINT TECHNOLOGY TO DECISION MAKING NEEDS

It is common to hear people complain that despite having masses of information available to them, they find it very hard to figure out what is going on.

Perhaps what they are really saying is, our company has brought in a range of 'point' technologies which give us information about something specific, but we find it very hard to 'abstract' from this what we need to know to make decisions.

Discussions about organisation digital technology often focus on such point technologies, such as a new sensor which can measure water quality after it leaves a water treatment plant, or devices to better monitor CO2 emissions.

We have some amazing 'point' technologies in 2020. New laptops for under £200 with so many different devices. Amazing sensors, fast data communication capabilities, vast cheap cloud storage, data visualisation systems, data analytics capability.

But consider what is necessary to get value from these investments. The sewage company can only use the data from its new water sensor if it serves the decision making of its maintenance and quality team, who already have a range of data sources to determine how well the systems are working, what maintenance is needed most urgently, and make a work schedule for maintenance workers. Do they really need more data, and what in particular would they do with it?

Or consider the company with a new CO2 emission monitoring device. While reducing CO2 may be a key objective, it needs to fit with whatever else the company is doing, heating a building or running a bus fleet, all tasks which cannot be done (usually) without CO2 emission. Any choices about reducing CO2 need to be balanced against the impact it may have on the company to do its fundamental tasks.

CONNECTING MANY DIFFERENT VARIABLES

Good map making can connect together hundreds of different variables and moving parts in a complex organisational working environment.

To illustrate this, consider how complex some of our home situations would look, such as buying family groceries, if we wanted to manage them purely with technology. While we may not have a deep understanding of other people's jobs other than the one we do ourselves, we can see that they are a real world task like our home situation, but scaled up in terms of money, complexity and risk.

The goal of family shopping is to keep kitchen cupboards and fridge stocked up so it has whatever our family might want readily available, while minimising cost and waste. To plan our purchases, we need to know what we currently have, make some estimation of what the consumption rate will be, consider the future consumption rate, and other risks such as having perishable goods left in our home when we are going away for a few days. We may do this for 100 items, and do it all in our heads.

There are 'point' technologies which could assist us. For example Amazon makes buttons we can press which will automatically re-order toilet roll. A data scientist could make a model of our milk consumption using past data, including the variability, how this changes depending on other factors, which we could use to predict how much milk to buy. But these would only help with two different items, and there are 100 items on our list.

Whether we have such point technologies or not, what we really need is a map, gathering together all the available data and telling us if our shopping list is right.

When we buy groceries, this map can be held in our heads. We don't need to discuss it with anyone else. But in an industrial situation, with other people involved, company procedures to follow, the map needs to be shared with others.

WELL MAPPED TECHNOLOGY IS LIKE A GREAT PERSONAL ASSISTANT

Like a great personal assistant, well mapped technology can tell you exactly what you need to know, when you need to know it, with all of the data perfectly crunched and arranged to get whatever insights you need.

A (human) personal assistant can do this because this person has a detailed understanding of the map of how you work, what you need, what is important and what is not.

In this sense, well mapped technology could be considered a form of artificial intelligence, because it provides a service which looks like something a person might provide.

It could be much better than a personal assistant – since personal assistants are not usually recruited for their map making abilities.

THINKING ABOUT DIGITAL ARCHITECTURE LIKE AN ARCHITECT

An architect, the kind who design buildings, needs to be a great map maker. The fundamental role is to create buildings which work for people, making a plan which connects the different elements together, including the pre-existing maps held by the client about what the building should look like, or ideas by the construction company about how it should be built. This map then needs to be fully understood by everybody.

In the building architecture world, while aesthetics is important, the practicality of the building is perhaps more important. A building should give us everything we need without any trouble. Such as how it holds in heat, the layout of the rooms, whether we can get the economic value we want from a commercial building.

A building architect has multiple issues to consider which all need to come together in a coherent whole. Temperature and light management, room size, location, client demands, and many different possible materials and building methods to choose from. The aim is to make a map for an end result which satisfies everybody as far as possible.

THE BUSINESS MODEL OF MAP MAKING

Opacity has a clear business model – or to put it another way, there can be good commercial reasons to keep things opaque.

Technology companies want you to believe their products will solve your problem and not ask too many more questions about it. People who have comfortable jobs or service contracts don't necessarily want to make it easier for others to see exactly what they do. An opaque world can discourage new entrants to the field.

In our commercial world, map makers can only beat opaquers if they have a better business model.

The strongest argument is that organisations with better maps can better meet their overall goals.

That argument only works if the people who care most about overall goals – the senior managers – are interested enough in digital technology to find out which technology has the best chance to reach the goals. Also they take the effort to listen to listen to map makers, not just their usual service providers or IT staff, who may have other objectives. This is increasingly happening, but perhaps not enough.

To succeed, map makers also need the support of people who use software to make their day to day decisions, who we call domain experts in this book. The ideas of mapmaking are completely orientated around serving these people, which makes this task easier. But also domain experts may not be comfortable getting into discussions around digital technology.

DRIVING A BETTER CONVERSATION ABOUT THE MAP

Organisational map makers need to get discussions going within the company about what path technology should take, and encourage others to be open about expressing their demands and what they find hard to understand.

A map making discussion is essentially talking about what works and what doesn't. Like talking about strategies for your football team, or which route to drive your car.

It is easy to imagine a group of doctors, teachers, engineers, IT professionals, talking about what does and doesn't help them in their work, and these conversations happen comfortably all the time, from workplace corridors to business conferences and online discussions.

But it is actually very rare to see domain experts talking about what digital technology will help them and what doesn't. This may be because in the past, someone else decided what technology people would use. Or because they do not feel they know enough about technology to discuss it.

It should be possible to talk about technology without having an in-depth knowledge of how it works, as a car driver does not need to know how an engine works to talk about a car. And it is also hard to combine a granular understanding of how technology works with a broader understanding of how it serves the organisation's goals.

MAP MAKING IN ORGANISATIONS – SOME NON-TECHNICAL PERSPECTIVES

HOW ORGANISATIONS PURSUE GOALS

When we are planning digital technology implementations, we need to have a clear idea of what we are trying to do and what we want to achieve for the organisation. So that should align with the organisation's goals.

Organisations have many goals, but they all roll down from the top key objectives, to try to improve the current situation in specific areas, without losing any ground. The basic strategy for doing this is set by the leaders, and passed on to the decision makers and planners in the organisation, whose role it is to make progress towards the goals through the decisions and plans they make. Digital technology does not usually pursue goals by itself.

In its normal activity, the organisation hires people, buys things, and does something with its people and things to make an output, which is sold or provided to someone.

Decisions along the way are made by domain experts, who are also looking for ways to do it better.

For example, for the core activities, the domain experts make decisions about the best schedule or way to deploy people and assets, and monitor how well it is being done.

There are support functions to this activity provided by other domain experts, such as financial management, IT / cybersecurity, risk management, asset management and maintenance.

Where a company sells something, domain experts maintain an understanding of the changing needs and desires of markets and individual customers.

The domain experts, as experienced professionals, have established methods to achieve the organisation's goals, such as the means that a safety manager uses to assess how well the company is following safe working practises.

This leads us to the map of familiar digital projects and systems providing tools and insights for domain experts in different roles. Such as people resource management, purchasing, supply chain management, planning / project management, scheduling, financial / accounting, risk management, asset management, maintenance management, security, customer relationship management.

DIGITAL MAPS NEED EFFECTIVE GOALS

If we are going to make a map for a digital implementation, we need a clear idea of where the map is meant to take us – that's the organisation's goals.

Map makers probably would not be setting goals, but they can get an understanding of how effective the goals are.

Goals are better if they converge rather than diverge – such as if you can improve environmental performance and achieve better sales at the same time, rather than when spending more on safety threatens to make the company unviable by increasing costs.

Having fewer goals makes it easier for an organisation to orient around the goals, and avoid conflict between goals.

MAP MAKING IN MULTIPLE DIRECTIONS

Map making is easiest to understand as a concept if we talk about it as something which is developed in only a forward direction, building out from the organisational goals and then adding in more and more detail.

But in digital technology projects, we are not able to do this, because we need to work with all the maps which already exist, in people's heads, and in the technology products which are already being used.

We can explain this with the analogy of someone making a new geographical map to achieve some new purpose. The map will draw on material in the existing maps, from other data, and perhaps from discussions with people about how they think their part of the world works and what they think should be included.

Some of the work might be adding more detail to what people already know. You already know one path which will take you to the church, but this map shows several others.

But some of the work might be reducing the amount of information. There are three different types of church in this village, but people don't really care much about what type of church they are. It is enough to just say there is a church, and use the same symbol for it. This can be called "abstracting".

In digital technology projects, abstracting is very important because there is so much information overload.

Imagine making a dashboard for an operations manager of a hospital. The hospital has enormous amounts of data being generated all the time – patients, staff, facilities, purchases, patient pipelines. The map maker has to find a way to abstract this data to give the operations manager only what is needed to work towards the goals.

DOMAIN EXPERTS CONTRIBUTE TO MAP MAKING

Domain experts have maps in their minds about what is happening, which evolve all the time.

Their expertise enables them to build maps quickly of a new situation, such as a doctor understanding a new contagious disease, or a trader understanding a new market situation. The capacity to do this could actually be the most valuable part of the expertise. For example, the most valuable trader may be the one who can quickly understand (map) a changed situation.

Domain experts are likely to have good contributions to make about digital map making. They know what digital information would be most helpful to them. If they are digitally competent, they may want to set up their own analytics systems, dashboards and software configurations, in effect doing their own digital mapping.

While domain experts are good at understanding the map of how to achieve goals in their domain, they are not necessarily good at explaining this map to others. This task has never been demanded of them. This is equivalent to asking an artist to explain how they do their work to someone else.

Within our own heads, we do not need to have any structure for knowledge. Our minds structure knowledge by themselves. One day we feel our minds have all kinds of disorganised thoughts, the next morning all of this knowledge has somehow organised it self in our heads and we can retrieve what we need effortlessly. We have made an internal map, even if we don't need to think about how it works.

SHIPPING COMPANY EXAMPLE

Here's an example of how we might build a digital twin for a shipping company (the organisation, not the physical ship).

The domain experts would be the superintendents, operations managers, technical and quality managers, safety managers, maintenance managers, purchasing managers, financial managers, fleet managers.

We can map out the information which they all work with to maintain their situation awareness, and where it comes from. Some of this information will overlap. For example, a technical manager decides that a vessel needs an engine overhaul by a certain date. This then brings in the crew, superintendents, operations managers, safety managers, maintenance managers, purchasing managers, financial department and fleet managers, all involved in different ways.

The inputs might also come from e-mails and forms, as well as digital data. Connecting e-mails into a digital model is very difficult, but a challenge worth tackling, since much of company information is still in e-mail format.

This information map can be the framework for a "organisational digital twin".

BUILDING CONSTRUCTION EXAMPLE

In the domain of building construction, the domain experts can be the bank lending decision maker, the developer, the architect, the engineer, the project manager, the construction company, the builder.

Each has different mental models and needs for situation awareness to update them. The banker's lending requirements, the developer's sense of what building would be most commercially valuable, the architects knowledge about the neighbourhood and the rough cost of different building options, the planning requirements, and the various options for how the building should be designed, including materials, energy management, room layout, roof.

The engineer has situation awareness about the planned building design, how to calculate if the design works and suggest improvements, plus regulatory requirements. Also an understanding of technical performance of various materials and equipment over the expected building's lifetime.

The project manager has situation awareness about the current construction schedule and budget, factors likely to impact this, and what can be done about them. Also the current approach of the people involved in the work and whether this is satisfactory. The construction company has situation awareness about different costs, and how to maximise the margin. The builder has situation awareness about where the building currently is and what needs to be done.

All of these people include past experiences in their situation awareness – what sort of developers defaulted on loans, what kinds of buildings sold well, what building designs worked or didn't work, technical problems with past buildings over their decades of life, previous problems with projects, reasons for cost overruns.

WHERE MAPMAKING GETS CHALLENGING

Domain experts often do not have a clear idea of what they need to know. If they did, 'information overload' problems would be easy to solve.

So someone else has to figure this out for them.

This leads to the hardest part of digital map making, what we could describe as 'modelling' – building models of what people need to know to build up their situation awareness.

[The words mapping and modelling can be interchangeable, but here we use the term modelling to describe the process of getting an abstracted or simplified picture of something].

CAR DRIVER SUPPORT SYSTEMS ANALOGY

An example of modelling is the design of the systems in a car to support the driver.

The largest "information service" to the driver is the large pane of glass in front of the driver's eyes. The rear view mirror and side mirrors are positioned so you barely need to move your head to see them. You can hear the noises of vehicles around you.

The digital services are designed to compliment this, not distract the driver from it. The most important information gets the highest priority.

Look slightly downwards and you see the most important information first – your speed, your remaining fuel, and perhaps some warning indications. There are digital audio warnings of indicators switched on, or an impending collision. Elements which do not directly impact safety, such as window controls or the radio, are positioned so they will not distract you, but are easy enough to find so you are not distracted looking for them.

This overall design, to support your situation awareness without distracting you, has been improved over the decades with enormous amounts of research. We can say that the car companies built up a sophisticated model of how the driver is best supported and least distracted, and mapped their technologies against this.

Similarly, organisational decision makers and domain experts need well thought through digital systems, modelled against their needs.

For example, a doctor gathers a mental picture of the health of a patient from a number of different monitoring devices. If the system is well set up, each device will give the doctor something useful, there will be warning alerts if something needs the doctor's immediate attention, and there will be no overloading of information.

The word "dashboard" is often used in the digital technology world – bear in mind that, as with a car, the "dashboard" is only part of the situation awareness.

Another challenge to technology companies is that every domain expert has different needs, while the needs of all car drivers are more or less the same.

And organisational domain experts also need different levels of information. The car dashboard provides only one layer of information – if we want to find out why we are getting an obscure warning, we need to go to a garage. But in an organisation, a warning to a doctor that someone's temperature is rising would lead the doctor to want to find out more about what might be happening, drilling into deeper layers of data.

Organisational decision makers might want their data to be presented in different abstracted ways. For example, someone in charge of monitoring public health in a small town might want to know how their numbers compare with the average for the country, and the average of other towns of a similar size.

ART AND MODELLING

Artists have large amounts of modelling in their work. Art often represents or describes something in our granular world, but taking a highly abstracted view, so it brings out important themes in our lives, separated out from day to day detail.

For example, an artist might describe life as an arc going from birth to death, rather than a challenge to get through each day.

An artist could describe a political belief, a historical event, a culture in abstract terms, so that we recognise instantly what is being described, without having to absorb so much detail.

Artists develop skills to communicate with minimum demands on our brain, such as when creating a piece of music with no more notes than it needs. This is a useful skill for map making – because where a map provides more information than is needed, it demands more of our scarce attention and focus.

JOURNALISTS' MAP MAKING SKILLS

Journalists have advanced map making skills of a certain sort. They can go into a situation, absorb a large amount of detail, and then distil it into a short story which tells someone else what is going on – in other words, they present an abstracted map.

Journalists are trained to focus on the 'why' of a story – why is it happening, what are the goals of the people making it happen – not just describe what is happening.

They develop skills to convey this story in a way which is easy to read. This doesn't necessarily mean writing it as if for a 7 year old, it can mean conveying a complex technical story in a way which someone with good intelligence, but no prior domain knowledge, can easily follow.

They do this by aligning what is happening with the knowledge structures in our brains, including where we currently are (what we already understand, what we want to know more about), and providing new information in a way which is easy to absorb.

They explain first why we should read something, what the benefits to us are of reading it, and what the most pertinent facts are, before we get into the detail. Then they only providing detail which is actually useful, not all the detail which is available.

Photo journalists may have skills in understanding where a photo adds something to the 'map' which the article presents.

TEXT BASED MAPS

The most common method for communicating maps in organisations is by written text, like this book, such as when companies write down their plans and how they propose to achieve them. But plenty of written maps are pretty poor at communicating.

We were never formally trained in this vital organisational skill, we are only formally trained in grammar. Correct grammar alone does not make written text a good map.

A good written map should orientate around the goal, why we are doing this. It is hard to get engaged in something if you have not been first shown why it should be done.

We could separate elements of the map in the text, such as the reason something is going to be done, the facts which underly this, and then the pathway for getting there. As we get into the detail, we can structure what we are saying, so we are not presenting multiple elements of understanding together, or being abstracted and detailed at the same time. Information which is already widely known can be separated from the main description of the map, or not included.

We should not assume that everyone accepts something is necessary or a rule must be followed, if this may be not the case. You should not describe a specific problem without saying why it is a problem.

A domain expert reading the map may wish to quickly understand the potential obstacles, such as any conflicts which may arise between people involved, so the 'meat' of the plan should be as easy to grasp as possible.

Within a map, technology should be described in terms of what it can do, rather than what it is. Otherwise you are contributing to the opacity. For example, a firewall is actually a software method of observing information packages with certain characteristics. It is not a wall and probably should not be understood as such.

Technical discussions should be presented so that a lack of technical understanding is not an obstacle to understanding the plan. You don't necessarily need to understand how an AI system works to understand what the goal of it is, and judge whether that makes sense.

TECHNOLOGIES WHICH CAN BE USED WITH MAP MAKING

Low code, digital twins, graph models and cloud data management.

Low code, digital twins, graph models and cloud data management are technologies which could be particularly useful in map making.

With low code technology a computer creates code automatically, from being given a map of how the software should work. If we need to update this map, the code automatically updates.

So there is no opacity. If we understand the map, we know what the code is doing, and have all the understanding we need.

No programming skill is needed. The focus of development work can go into the map making, rather than the coding, as usually happens.

Looking at the "digital twin". It has an established product 'map' in the technology industry, as a digital replica of an asset in the real world. It is a product explicitly to support someone's situation awareness, telling them what is happening with the asset.

Digital twins are not usually designed to dovetail with the mental models and situation awareness which domain experts currently have, or need. But they could be.

The graph model is a means of connecting together multiple data sources by how the data affect each other.

Consider the different devices a doctor might use when monitoring the health of a patient in intensive care, all generating their own data. At the moment, the only place these different data sources come together is in the doctor's head, which means that the data is not providing any overall insight into the patient's condition by itself.

Cloud data management services are when a company provides a service to gather and manage data and make it available to other software applications. It sits on top of the cloud data storage services provided by companies like AWS. For map makers, it means a lot of the difficult data technical work is handled by someone else, so does not distract from the map making task.

THE DIGITAL TWIN

Looking further at the 'digital twin', the digital 'replica' of something in the real world. As a software concept, it is typically applied in heavy industry – ships, offshore oil platforms, manufacturing plants – where the real things are highly complex, with a lot of different data sources. It is difficult for a person to understand what is going on.

The idea is that a detailed and accurate digital replica of a real asset can give domain experts situation awareness of what is happening.

Digital twins are made up of a mixture of static data (such as about the asset's design and construction), and dynamic data (something which has changed, such as recent survey data showing the extent of corrosion, or operational data from sensors and control systems). It may also include modelling and analytic capability.

In theory, we can use it to find out what is going on, what is going to happen, and what might happen if we were to take a certain course of action. So everything can operate at peak efficiency and reliability, accidents never happen, and maintenance work is done neither too early nor too late.

The problem many digital twin projects encounter is the challenge of managing the resolution of it, and the cost. A high resolution replica – perhaps with all possible data available – would be theoretically possible to build, but would come at infinite cost. A low resolution replica could be made very easily – perhaps just a simple static model – but would not provide much insight. Most 'digital twins' in use today are still fairly static models.

Connecting to the domain expert's mental "twin"

We could evolve the idea to construct digital twins which are aligned with the expert's mental models.

By this, we mean the mental models we all build in our minds about our situation and what is happening in them. In prehistoric times, we built mental models of our relationships with other tribe members, our food supplies, our enemies and the threats. Today we build mental models of our organisations and machines. Our models include what is happening now, where we would like to be, and what changes we think we could make to what is happening now which would take us there.

We could use the same terminology and call our mental models "mental twins".

By planning to align digital twins and mental models, it could be easier to work out what would be valuable to include in the digital twins, helping us make our technology investments make more value and avoid wasted effort.

We could adapt the idea to domains where situation awareness is important but there are no specific physical assets, such as cyber-security (to identify weaknesses in our security defences), supply chain management (to identify emerging problems), or safety (to identify new hazards).

Managing our own "mental twin ROI"

With our mental modelling, we have no problem working out how much effort to invest in building it to make a return. We are good at working out how much we need to know and understand about a situation, including what is happening now and what might happen.

We are also good at judging when to try predicting what is going to happen. In our personal lives, we often do not predict at all, because we know that it is so difficult to do. We would probably not try to predict, for example, how much milk we will have left in the fridge in a week, or what our children's grades will be. We learn instead the importance of being aware of what is going on right now.

Perhaps this is a useful lesson for the digital twin world, and the digital maps behind it. There are lots of effort going into making digital twins which can predict difficult things, such as the rate of degradation of a machine. Are we trying too hard to predict things digitally?

GRAPH MODELS

Graph modelling is a sensible partner to digital map making, as a digital technology which can connect together many different forms of information without a rigid structure, similarly to how information connects together in the real world.

The graph model can enable an understanding of what the data actually indicates in the real world, and its importance, to be persisted through to the information structure. It means that any discussion about the accuracy, security or performance of the data can be easily connected to the wider organisational purpose, rather than just talking about data as data.

The value proposition of a graph model is to bring the right knowledge to the right person at the right time. Or it can trigger the right automated response, or sequence of responses. It can be aligned with the 'domain logic', how people normally work with this data.

It provides an alternative to relational databases, which are used to hold most digital information today. These hold data like a spreadsheet does, in tables with rows and columns.

Real world data does not fit easily in spreadsheets. As an example, consider your drive to work. You have many loosely connected elements. The time you need to leave, the roads you could take, how congestion changes at different times and days, particular issues happening today such as road works, an urgent meeting, or an appointment elsewhere before work.

With a graph model, we can connect together all of these data sources to bring the right information to the right person at the right time. You could be informed about your meetings and the best route to their locations, changes in congestion and anything else relevant. This is quite a simple example, but someone's drive to work is probably the simplest part of their working day.

The graph model can overlay on top of other corporate digital systems, such as analytics / AI systems, and sensor based monitoring systems. In this way, it can help people get more value out of their investment in them.

They can capture 'adjacency' – such as what to look at more carefully when something else happens, or what should happen after something else happens.

The graph models can bring different information to different people, depending on their role. They can work with mobile apps, and give people alerts at appropriate times.

If a graph model is well constructed, aligning with how people already work and think, it can make digital technology feel less complex. This is in the same way that car technology does not feel complex, if it only tells you what you need to know, and does not confuse you.

It is also possible to integrate different graph models together. Imagine if you made multiple graph models for a car, such as for the passenger compartment, the frame, drive train and systems (brakes, cooling, suspension). The models can be gradually developed and integrated together using graph models. They are easily extensible and maintainable.

Graph models can be easily built to budget. The more data integrations or granularity it has, the more expensive it is to build, but conversely you can build a cheaper model with less features.

WORKING WITH DATA

Underlying all digital technology is the data sources. It will be much easier to incorporate data into your mapped out digital systems if the data itself is in good order.

If you think of the map like a plumbing system in your house, it will be much easier to manage if it connects directly to a supply of clean municipal tap water, rather than if you have to go down the street with a bucket to a handpump, providing water with varying reliability and quality. This could be a fair analogy to the challenges of getting data from different data sources today.

While mapmakers might not be engaged with data management projects, it helps if they can recognise well managed data.

Well managed data would probably have consistent naming conventions, consistent data quality, rules, and secure systems for sharing it. It will be easy to integrate the various data sources or services, via straightforward APIs (Application Programming Interfaces).

Conversely, you might find yourself having to try to integrate your systems with sensors with difficult APIs, other software packages from software companies who do not make data sharing easy, data which has been stored in 'historians' but with lots of data missing, or data which is wrongly indexed, such as having a time stamp which is 10 seconds out, so it is very hard to integrate with other data on the basis of time.

Often you might not know how good the data is until you start looking at it. This would be justification for an 'agile' working method, where you work continually on an experimental basis, testing out projects on a small scale before putting bigger resources into them.

CLOUD DATA MANAGEMENT

One group of services which can really help is cloud data management, where a service company takes on the task of integrating with multiple data sources, gathering and storing data on a cloud service, and managing its quality.

They sometimes contextualise, putting together related data, so it is easier for a software system downstream to access a package of related data streams and understand what they all mean.

This means that good data can be easily available to other software packages, if they are authorised to access it by the data owner.

These services were set up mainly with sensor data in mind, but are increasingly being used to manage data from software packages. This is important when data from one software system is used as part of someone else's task, such as where one person is planning what maintenance work to do, and another is making sure the necessary spare parts and people are available to do it.

In our own domain of shipping and oil/gas, we have seen a number of cloud data management service providers, including DNV Veracity, MAN / Mya, Cognite and Kongsberg Digital.

These services manage data both from sensor systems and from other software systems.

As of 2020, cloud technologies are in favour with investors, who have seen how reliant everybody was on cloud technologies during the Covid period, so may think cloud technologies are invincible as an investment proposition.

Having well managed cloud data also makes life easier for smaller software companies to offer a useful service doing a specific task, where previously they would have needed to be very large to have access to the necessary data. It makes it theoretically possible for a customer to work with many software providers all doing one small task.

If data is stored in standardised formats, software companies compete on how useful their software tools are, which can unlock a lot of value for the market. It should also be easier to switch from one software tool to another but maintain your data.

And the ease of sharing data with cloud data storage systems is motivating the development of more data standards, which need cross industry collaboration.

THE OPAQUING STRATEGIES

The opposing force to mapmaking, is when people's actions, or lack of actions, make technologies harder to understand. We call this opaquing. (You could also call it obfuscating).

Explaining something and making it clear is hard work, which people don't want to do without good reason. So this leads to opacity by default. But why don't people see reason to explain the technology?

People talk about technology products as though implementing them was a goal in itself, rather than talking about how technology serves the company's goals. Such as when someone says that the company needs more "AI". Note that AI can be an extremely opaque technology, with no clear definition, often provided with big promises attached and no understanding of how it will achieve them.

Technology enthusiasts may opaque to avoid the effort of working out, and engaging with people, on a pathway to install technologies in an organisational structure.

If we are dealing just with such "point" technologies, map making is unnecessary. We don't need a map for how an antivirus software works. But we do need a map for how an organisation is going to get value from antivirus software, ensuring all the PCs have up to date virus definitions, their systems are scanning every file which is entered onto the network.

The organisation will probably have an expert in charge of cyber-security, who has bought a number of such "point" products. But without a clear map of how the products fit together, it will be very hard to solve any problem, such as identifying where the hole is in the organisation's cybersecurity structure which allowed a certain hack to get through.

Senior managers may inadvertently be opaquing, when they talk about the need for digitalisation without being specific about what they think should be digitalised, instead perhaps saying that we need an "agile culture" so we might figure it out through experimentation.

This is unusual behaviour for a senior manager. In other fields, it would be normal for a manager to state how their goal might be reached – such as how they propose to increase sales or reduce accidents.

While agile and experimentalism can be an important part of digitalisation projects, it should not be the main driving force. We need to know where we are trying to get to.

Perhaps senior managers do not have a clear idea themselves of which technologies would best serve their organisation. Here our framework of orientating around situation awareness may help.

Perhaps senior managers see the big technology companies as the digitalisation leaders, and are only copying what they say. But big tech companies do not have much of an incentive to give clear digitalisation goals. All of their customers are different and have different goals. Many tech companies like to treat their customers as all the same, believing that it is not their role to provide software customised to any particular customer. Sometimes there seems to be a culture of copying what the big tech companies do.

The big tech organisations do not differentiate their customers much, if at all, in the sense that everybody gets the same Amazon website. This is not a problem for Amazon, since it does not offer any customised service for domain experts. But your company's digital technology probably does, or should do. A domain expert would not be using Amazon for company purchases, unless they know exactly what they want to buy.

Treating all customers the same means that from the domain expert's perspective, the technology only makes sense if it is perfectly aligned with what you want. The software's map is the same as your map. Otherwise you are left trying to work out what the map of the software is.

Bear in mind that good digitalisation projects do not necessary require big investments in digital products - the right digital solution may be based on shared forms and files, which is not easy, but can be done with Google Documents.

We may be able to explain how to get more value from data with simple stories rather than talking about big technology products. For example, in the maritime industry, people understand that an accident report is likely to be more accurate if written by an engineer onboard a ship, rather than a junior person in the office quality department. Or that defect reports commonly say that the cause was crew negligence, because crew negligence is the only defect covered by the company's insurance.

Other drivers for opacity can be psychological, such as where technology enthusiasts make technology sound more complex than they need to, because they think it bolsters their position in the company, or it discourages people with lesser deep technical knowledge from sharing their point of view.

SOME GOVERNMENTS LIKE OPACITY

The Chinese and Russian governments are opaque compared to most Western ones. They do not want people to have the understanding they would need to ask detailed questions. Their strategy is to divert attention onto what is going well, and suppress voices which show that the map is not what it seems.

They place very little value on curiosity, people's desire to understand how things work. They are happy to use technology itself to spread opacity.

The Russian government, or entities acting on its behalf, have world leading competence in hacking, while pretending that it is not them doing it. The goal of the hacking appears to be to spread opacity around the world, seeding distrust in institutions. They particularly dislike institutions which aim to create maps, such as high quality independent news outlets.

The Chinese government is delighted to show that it is a world leader in technology, particularly AI and 5G, which are themselves very opaque technologies. They develop their technology capability doing tasks which Western governments are capable of doing, but would not usually do, such as using face recognition, credit scores and mobile phone tracking apps to control people.

On the other side, there are forces for mapmaking in Russia and China, and forces for opaquing in Europe and the US. But different elements typically end up on top.

WINNING WITH BETTER CONVERSATIONS

Opaquers can be extremely good story tellers, talking about wonderful things which technology can do, which can close down discussion about how the technology works.

A mapmaker in contrast opens up the discussion about how it works, and encourages domain experts to talk about what they do, their goals, and what works for them. Perhaps, in the end, encouraging the right conversation is the best way to win.

The number of people in the world who can explain digital technology without resorting to technobabble, and focussing on what technology can do, rather than what it is, is very small. The need is very big. By developing the skill yourself, you also encourage it from others.

Here's some more examples of value adding digital mapmaking conversations. For school lighting, we can make a map showing the best time to change to LED bulbs, showing how it could be done, what the costs and benefits would be. In shipping, we can make maps showing the best time to clean a ship hull, before the growth on it gets so much that cleaning gets difficult.

We could use maps to make travelling by public transport almost as fast and convenient as travelling by car, if we had vehicles arriving at times when they were most needed, connections between modes happening very quickly, and a capacity for operators to know exactly when one connection should be delayed waiting for another one, to achieve the minimum impact for all passengers.

Western companies can compete with Chinese companies, by creating working environments which people are much happier in, offering their best selves and most creative abilities. Working with well-mapped digital technology, which supports situation awareness and continuous learning, is more enjoyable.

Map making vs opaquing is a timeless theme for humanity – and should now become a theme of the technology world too, as it becomes more pervasive in our lives.

Contact the author Karl Jeffery on jeffery@d-e-j.com